Project 7-11

Starting out in Reading and Writing

Book 1

Sheila Lane and Marion Kemp

for 7-8 year olds

1 Meet Tom, Lucy and Jan

What's your name?
▶ Write your name in here.

This activity book is for:

    thinking   listening   reading   writing

What kind of books do you like best?
▶ Write in here.

What else do you like doing?
▶ Write in here.

 When you see this drawing it means go through this page with a grown-up.

Sometimes you will see this:

Write the title of the book you are reading this week.

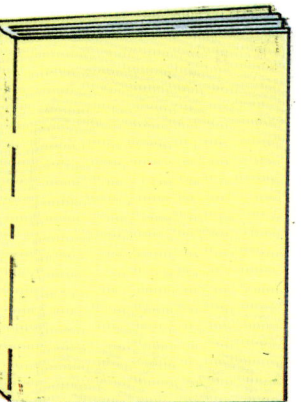

This means fill in the book cover.

Sometimes we suggest books for you to read.

Have you read . . . ?

Write **yes** or **no** in here. ☐

This tells you to use your notebook for the next activity.

When you see this:

it means write a story on a piece of paper.

2 What's it about?

"What do you think this book is about? Is it about...tigers... crocodiles... or penguins?"

▶ Fill in the word.

I think this book is about _____

The title of a book is written on the outside of the front cover.

▶ Write a title on the cover of each book.

 "My favourite book is Jokes and Riddles."

 "Ask me one."

 "Why did the sausage roll?"  "Because it was pushed!"

Write the title of the book you are reading this week.

Here is a **page** from the inside of a book about shapes.

The title for the page could be

_____

▶ Write a title for this page. The title for this page could be _____

_____

_____

▶ Fill in the name of the **set** for each sentence.

1 Blue, red, yellow and green are all _____

2 Doll, pedal-car and teddy-bear are all _____

3 Shirt, vest, hat and coat are all _____

4 Robin, sparrow and eagle are all _____

Write the titles of some of the books in your home.

Can you find 10 titles . . . or more?

3 Nasty...and nice

Would you rather be ... covered in jam ... soaked in water ... or ... pulled through the mud by a dog?

▶ Finish the sentence:
The worst for me _____
_____

▶ Draw a picture of:

slug stew   mashed worms   spider dumplings

Which would you rather be made to eat?

▶ Make a list of some of the worst things that could happen to you.

The worst things for me are...
_____
_____
_____
_____

Have you read this book?

Write **yes** or **no** in here.
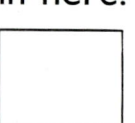

Write the title of the book you are reading this week.

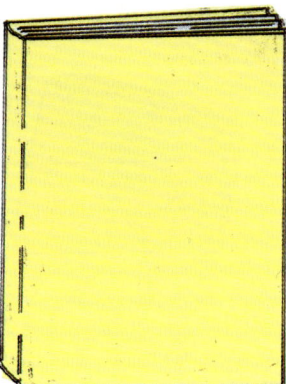

Favourite things

▶ Fill in the missing words.

1 Lucy's favourite flavour is __chocolate__.
2 _____ is her second favourite.
3 The flavour in third place is _____.
4 _____ is only in fifth place.
5 Lucy's least favourite flavour is _____.

▶ Make a list of **your** favourite flavours.

▶ Make a list of **your** favourite games.

Write three headings:

doing   seeing   hearing

Write your favourites under each one.

4 A read-and-write story

The Hungry Mouse

Some of the story is missing.
▶ Read the story and write the missing parts.

Mouse lived in a little cupboard at the Town Hall. One night she was feeling so hungry that she decided to

What a sight met her eyes! There on the table were

So Mouse feasted all day. How she enjoyed the

But she did not notice that, as she ate and ate, her stomach got

Next morning, when the Town Hall clock struck 6, she decided to return to her nest in the cupboard. BUT

▶ Go on with the story here.

_____
_____
_____
_____

"Now how shall I get out of here?"

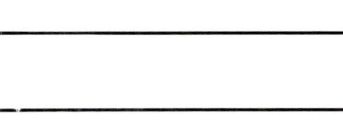

Now write your own story. Think of a title and write it here:

_____
_____

5 What's missing?

▶ Draw in all the missing wheels. What else is missing?
Write the missing word in each sentence.

1 The ___leg___ of the dog is missing.
2 The _____ of the shop is missing.
3 The _____ of the clock is missing.
4 The _____ of the policeman is missing.
5 The _____ of the boy is missing.

▶ What pet is missing from each of these homes?
Write a sentence for each home like this:

1 <u>A dog is missing from the kennel.</u>
2 _____
3 _____

▶ Choose the right word for each sentence, like this:

1 The dog began to __eat__ his dinner.

2 A rabbit can _____ .

3 A fish can _____ in the sea.

4 A cat is _____ in the basket.

(eat kick) (fly hop) (walk swim) (lying flying)

▶ Complete the word for each picture.

snow __man__   egg_____   gold_____

lady_____   foot_____   hand_____

Word sums

hat flower light beam

▶ Write words beginning with sun.
__sunlight__ _____
_____ _____

Look! up + stairs = upstairs ▶ Do these:

down + stairs = __downstairs__   can + _____ = cannot

some + thing = _____   for + _____ = forgot

any + thing = _____   be + _____ = belong

be + side = _____   no + _____ = nothing

Notebook Look in your story books. Collect some more words which have two parts.

(I know! rain...) (...and bow.)

6 Who is it?

This is a page from a **turn over book**.

▶ Read the mixed up strips.

	He wears a dark jacket with smart buttons and a belt. Can you see a whistle in his pocket?
	Fireman Fred has a shiny helmet on his head when he goes to a fire. It is shaped like a bucket.
	They fit into his big, strong boots, which are black. Fred's boots stop the water from making his feet wet.
	His trousers are dark blue and he tucks the bottoms in.

▶ Now read the strips in the right order.
Write the story of Fred.

Fireman Fred has _____
_____
_____
_____
_____
_____

What am I?

▶ Read the riddles and write the answers.

I am made of wood.
I have arms but no legs.
Birds make their nests in me.
What am I?

I have a head,
a foot and four legs,
but I am not an animal.
You sleep in me at night.
What am I?

I am a tree

I am _____

I am yellow.
I twinkle in the night sky.
I am a friend to sailors.
What am I?

I am _____

I rise in the sky every morning.
I give light.
Sometimes I hide behind a cloud.
What am I?

I am _____

▶ Write a riddle in the shape below.

Do you know this joke?

When is a horse not a horse?

When it's a horseshoe!

Make a collection of riddles.
Read them to your friends.
Ask them to guess the answers.

7 Looking at pictures

Look at the picture. ▶ Write a title for the picture.

▶ Write **yes** or **no** in the box.

1 Can you see two policemen in the picture?
2 Has one of the policemen had an accident?
3 Has a child had an accident?
4 Was the child running after a ball?
5 Did the balloon burst?
6 Can you see an ambulance in the road?

▶ What are they saying? Write in the balloons.

What would you say to the child who ran into the road?

THE GREEN CROSS CODE

1 First find a safe place to cross, then stop.

2 Stand on the pavement near the kerb.

3 Look all round for traffic and listen.

4 If traffic is coming, let it pass. Look all round again.

5 When there is no traffic near, walk straight across the road.

6 Keep looking and listening for traffic while you cross.

▶ Put a piece of paper over the Code.
Test yourself by filling in the missing words.

1 First find a _____ place to cross, then stop.
2 _____ on the pavement near the kerb.
3 _____ all round for traffic and _____ .
4 If traffic is coming, let it _____ . Look all round _____ .
5 When there is no _____ near, walk straight across the _____ .
6 Keep _____ and _____ for traffic while you _____ .

Take the paper away.
How many missing words did you know?

▶ Read the **Alphabet Number Code**.

A	B	C	D	E	F	G	H	I	J	K	L	M	N	O	P	Q	R	S	T	U	V	W	X	Y	Z
1	2	3	4	5	6	7	8	9	10	11	12	13	14	15	16	17	18	19	20	21	22	23	24	25	26

What does 19 1 6 5 mean?

19 = s 1 = a
6 = f   5 = e
19 1 6 5 means SAFE

What does this code mean?

12 15 15 11	1 14 4	12 9 19 20 5 14

8 What can you see?

▶ Look at this book cover.
You can see ... one little fish,
one cloud in the sky
and **many** sea-birds.

So **sea-birds** are the most important and tell us what the book is about.

▶ Fill in the title on the book cover.

Here are 3 pictures. What is most important in each one?
▶ Draw a ring round the best title for each picture.

Dolls   Leaves   Birds
Toys   Fruits   Animals
Trains   Apples   Trees

Here are 3 sets of pictures. ▶ Fill in the name of each set.

1   These are all _____.
2   These are all _____.
3   These are all _____.

Here are 2 sentences. ▶ Fill in the name of each set.

1 Flats, houses and bungalows are all names of _____.

2 Oak, ash and elm are all names of _____.

The title of this picture could be:

'Shopping in the Rain'

'What a Day!'

'It's Raining Cats and Dogs'

▶ Draw a ring round the title you like best.

What else can you see in the picture?
▶ Fill in a number word for each sentence.

1 In the picture there are ____ men, ____ women and ____ children.

2 ____ people have umbrellas.

3 ____ people are carrying shopping baskets.

4 There are ____ dogs and ____ cat in the picture.

5 There are ____ bicycles by the fountain.

Can you see two little words in

SG ?

Draw a circle around any words you find in
STANDING
SITTING   WATCHING

Write the title of the book you are reading this week.

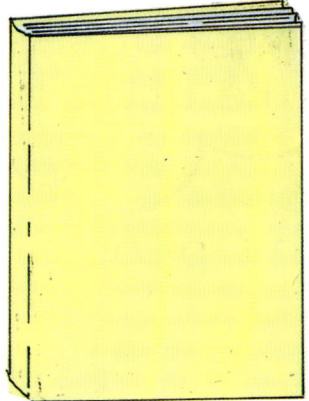

9 A read-and-write story

The Boy Who Flew Too Near The Sun

▶ Read the first part of the story.

Long, long ago, a boy flew up into the sky on wings made of birds' feathers stuck together with wax. As he flew up and up, far away above the clouds, he felt happy and full of joy.

What did the boy say as he flew up?
▶ Write his words in the clouds.

- I am flying up
- My wings are
- Now I am above
- I look like

What did the boy say as he flew down?
▶ Write his words in the clouds.

- Down below the houses look like little boxes.
- Fields look like
- Trees look like
- I feel so
- The people

▶ Read the next part of the story.

The boy flew on . . . up and up and up.
He flew nearer and nearer to the hot sun.

What did the boy say as he became very hot?
▶ Write his words.

▶ Read the next part of the story.

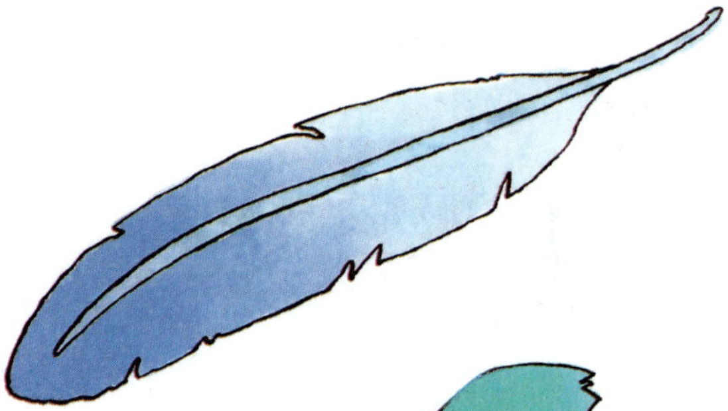

Soon the boy was so near to the sun that it began to melt the wax which was holding his wings together.
First one feather flew off . . .

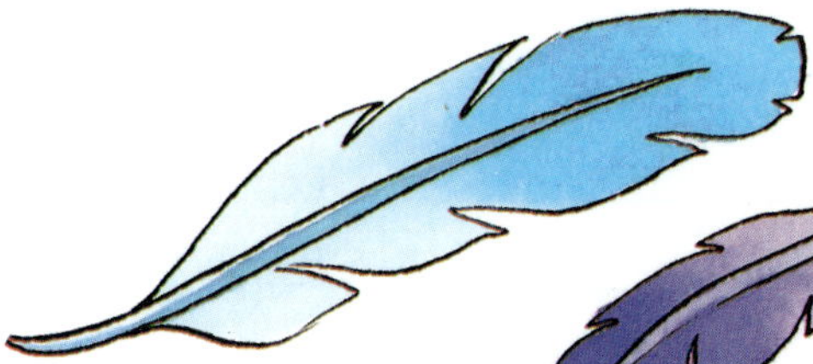

then another

then another.

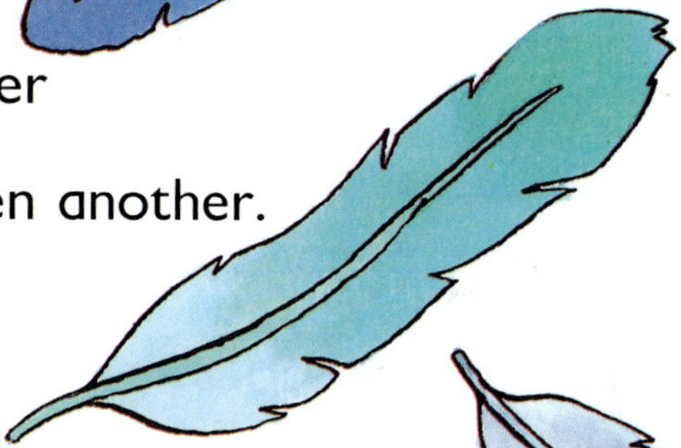

What did the boy say when he saw all the feathers flying around him?
▶ Write his words.

How do you think the story ended?

▶ Write here.

_____
_____
_____

10 Fun with words

Look at the food picture for 1 minute then cover it with a piece of paper.

▶ Write down how many of each food without looking at the picture again.

_____ eggs   _____ sausages   _____ tarts
_____ bananas _____ apples   _____ fish

The names of these foods are back to front.
▶ Write the correct spelling in the empty shape.

There are 10 names of food and drink hidden in the sausages.

▶ Write the names on the lines:

1 doughnut

2 _____

3 _____

4 _____

5 _____

6 _____

7 _____

8 _____

9 _____

10 _____

(sausages contain: shop, tomato, orange, egg, grapes, nut, doughnut)

▶ Fit the names from the box into the puzzle.

apple
apricot
bread ✓
egg
fish
kipper
rusk
sausage
toast

b	r	e	a	d
r				
e				
a				
k				
f				
a				
s				
t				

How many foods can you see in this basket? They are all on this page.

▶ Write the names here.

_____   _____

_____   _____

_____   _____

21

11 Did you know?

A thousand years ago, Christmas Day was called Adam and Eve's Day by some people. Adam and Eve Trees were decorated with apples, paper flowers and shining things. Five hundred years later, people in Germany began decorating their Christmas trees with ginger-bread biscuits, little wax angels and candles.

▶ Write the names of the 3 things which were put on the Adam and Eve Tree inside this tree.

▶ Write the names of the 3 things which were put on the German Christmas tree inside this tree.

What would you put on a Christmas tree?

Fill in the labels.

12 Opposites

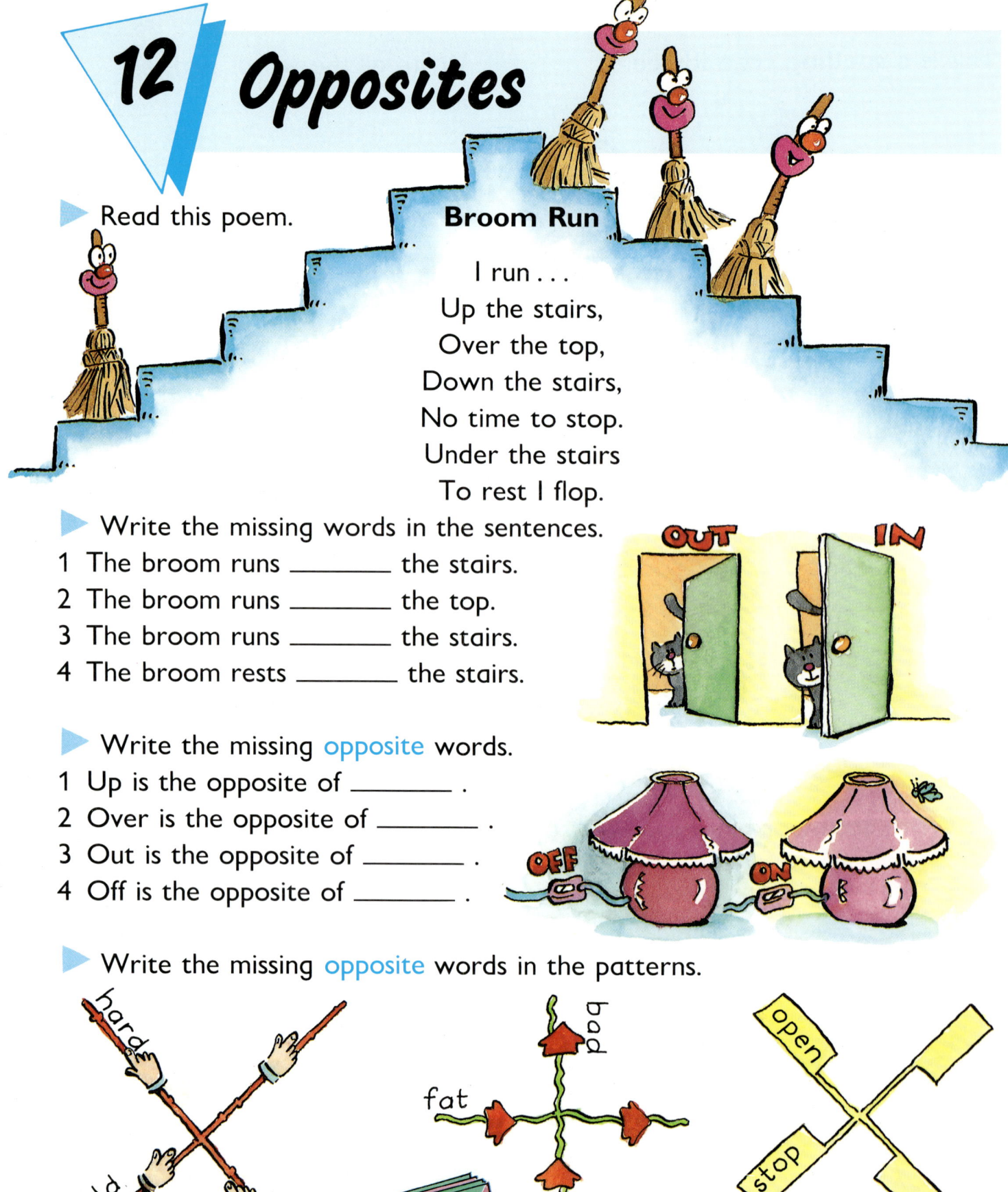

▶ Read this poem.

Broom Run

I run . . .
Up the stairs,
Over the top,
Down the stairs,
No time to stop.
Under the stairs
To rest I flop.

▶ Write the missing words in the sentences.
1 The broom runs _____ the stairs.
2 The broom runs _____ the top.
3 The broom runs _____ the stairs.
4 The broom rests _____ the stairs.

▶ Write the missing opposite words.
1 Up is the opposite of _____ .
2 Over is the opposite of _____ .
3 Out is the opposite of _____ .
4 Off is the opposite of _____ .

▶ Write the missing opposite words in the patterns.

hard / cold

bad / fat

open / stop

Make up some more opposite patterns of your own.

13 A read-and-write story

The Magic Powder

▶ Look at the pictures. Read the words in the balloons.
Write a sentence for each picture.

_____

_____

_____

_____

_____

_____

Think about how Pumpkin-Head comes to life.

What will his neck do?
How does he walk?
Will he begin to talk?

▶ Write about Pumpkin-Head coming to life.

_____
_____
_____

Perhaps Boy will want him for a friend.
Perhaps Old Mombi will want him to do the work.
Perhaps Pumpkin-Head will try to run away.

▶ Write about what happens next.

_____
_____
_____
_____

Mombi's Magic Powder could bring things to life.
What would you do with a box of Magic Powder?

Write a story on a piece of paper about: **My Box of Magic Powder** or draw a picture of one of your toys coming to life.

14 Names

"What's a forename?"

"A forename is someone's first name."

▶ Write your forename.

_____

Do you like your forename? Did you know that most forenames have special meanings?

Is *your* name here?

Angela means angel
Esther...star
Caleb...dog
Leroy...king
Iris...rainbow
Rose...rose
Oscar...spear
William...helmet
Robin...robin
Daisy...daisy

Choose 3 of the names. ▶ Write sentences to show what they mean.

_____

_____

_____

▶ Write 2 forenames which you would choose for yourself.

"Remember to use capital letters and full stops."

_____

_____

"Does a pet's name begin with a capital letter?"

"Yes! All special names begin with a capital letter."

▶ Give each of these pets a name.

_____   _____   _____

▶ Read this poem about a frog who was given some unkind nicknames.

The Frog

Be kind and gentle to the frog,
And do not call him names,
As 'Slimey Skin', or 'Polly-wog'
Or likewise, 'Ugly James'.

                      Belloc

Slimey Skin!

▶ Make up a nickname to describe these creatures.

I'm called _____   I'm called _____

Here is Magnus the dinosaur.

These 3 words describe Magnus:
1 huge   2 slow   3 old

This sentence describes Magnus: Magnus was a huge, slow, old dinosaur.

▶ Write 3 words to describe a puppy.

_____
_____
_____

Use the three words in a sentence to describe a puppy.

_____
_____
_____

Write the title of the book you are reading this week.

15 The Magic Wishing Tree

▶ Look at the pictures and read the words in the balloons. Write a sentence for each picture.

A wind blew in the leaves of the Magic Wishing Tree.

As soon as they opened their eyes, the children found themselves in a strange, grey, dusty place.

▶ Finish each of these sentences about what it was like.

When they looked round, they **saw** _____

_____

When they listened they could **hear** _____

_____

They could **smell** _____

The boy put out his hand and **touched** _____

_____

The girl said, "Look! Let's **taste** these _____

_____

Some time later...

I'm tired. Let's go back home to Earth now.

But how do we make a wish now we're on the moon?

Perhaps...
they found a magic moonstone,
or they rode down to Earth on a moon-beam,
or they made a moon spell,
or...

▶ Write about how the children wished themselves back to Earth.

_____

_____

_____

_____

_____

16 Story beginnings

▶ Write these story beginnings so that they make sense.

1 ago   Long   long
   Long, long ago

2 morning   Early   one
   _____

3 was   Once   there
   _____

4 the   across   sea   away   Far
   _____

▶ Finish the sentence for each picture.

When I heard the postman's knock...
I ran downstairs to the door.

I snuggled down into my bed...
_____

Looking down, the cat saw...
_____
_____

The children ran...
_____
_____

Look at these two pictures.

▶ Write some sentences to tell the next part of the story.

_____

_____

_____

_____

_____

_____

▶ Read the story beginnings on page 32. Look at the story beginning about the wizard on this page.

Choose the story beginning you like best.
Use it to begin your own story.

Once upon a time there was a wizard who lived inside a small, shiny lamp. Whenever anyone rubbed the lamp the wizard began to use his magic.

17 I spy

What can you spy with your little eye, beginning with s?
▶ Write the names here.

_____ _____ _____ _____

_____ _____ _____ _____

▶ Write **one** of the letters in the box at the beginning of each little word to make a new word.

____ and   ____ ill   ____ all   ____ and
____ ill   ____ all   ____ ill   ____ all

`h  b  w`

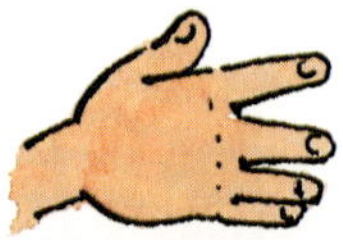

In your notebook draw:

a hand. Write **-and** words in the hand.

a wall. Write **-all** words in the wall.

a hill. Write **-ill** words in the hill.

a ring. Write **-ing** words in the ring.

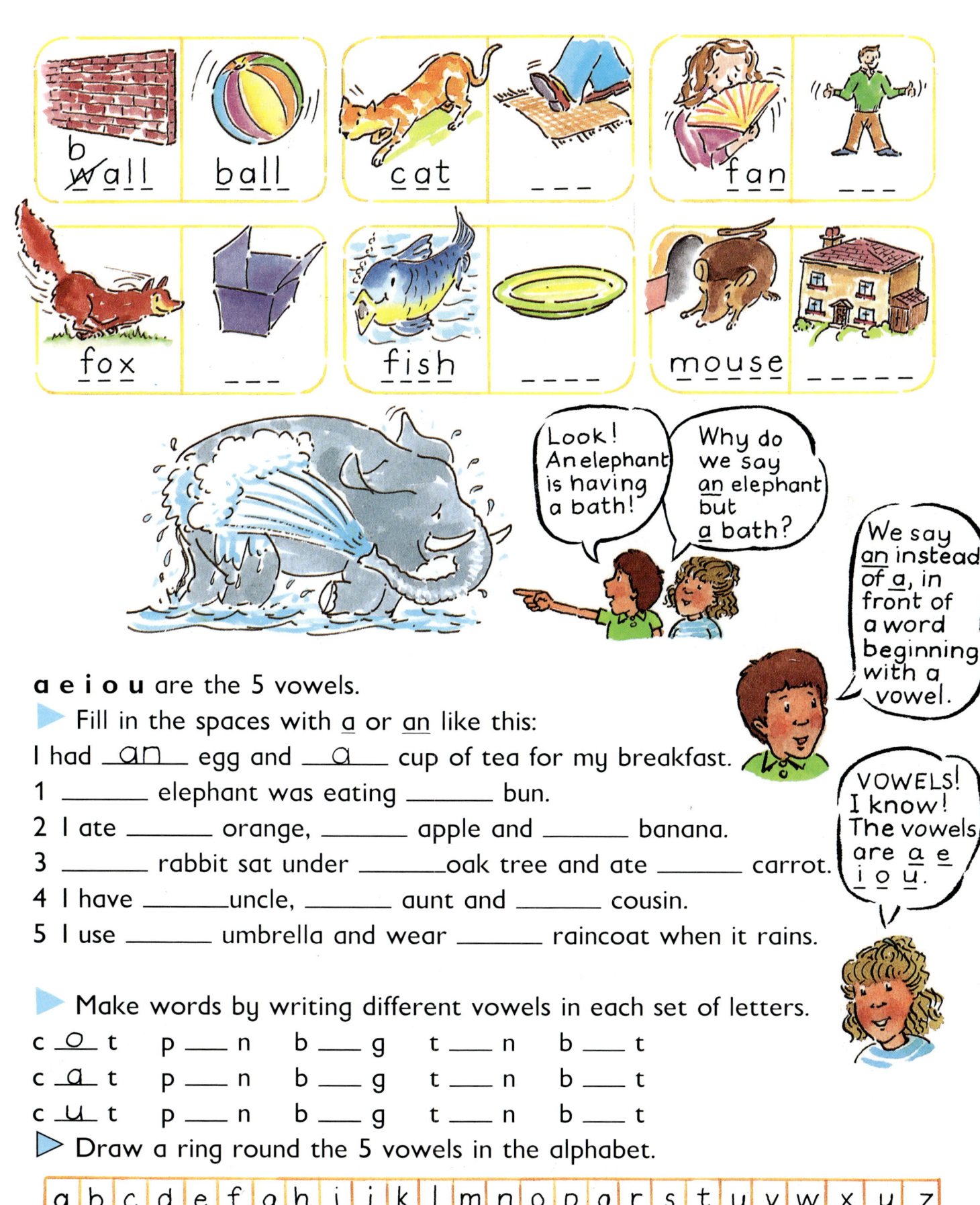

18 Who said it?

▶ Write a title for the picture. _____

Look at the picture. Find the old lady, the park-keeper and the children who are dropping sweet papers. ▶ Write down who you think said the words.

(I blame their mothers.)   (I spend all my time picking up litter.)   (Sorry, mister!)

The old lady.   _____   _____

Find the park-keeper who is angry with a dog. ▶ Write down who you think said the words.

(Can't you read?)   (But mister! Dogs can't read.)

_____   _____

Find the child who is poking a sleeper's hat off. ▶ Write down who you think said the words.

(Ooo! What was that?)   (Tweet! Tweet! It was just a little bird.)

_____   _____

Who might say this to you ... and when?      My father might say it when I leave the door open.

_____ might say it

when _____

_____ might say it

when _____

"Pick it up!"

_____ might say it

when _____

"Just look at the floor!"

_____ might say it

when _____

▶ Join the 2 short sentences to make 1 long sentence, using the word when.      "Remember to take away the first full stop."

1 I went to bed. I was tired.
   I went to bed when I was tired.

2 I opened the door. I heard a knock.
   _____

3 The bus stopped. I put up my hand.
   _____

4 My cat purred. I gave her some fish.
   _____

5 The bath began to fill. I turned the tap.
   _____

19 The alphabet

Did you ever see...

...an alligator in an apron...

...a beetle on a big, blue bicycle...

...a cat carrying a canary in a cage...?

What's a crocodile's favourite game?

Snap!

Make up some more like these:
 A <u>d</u>inosaur <u>d</u>oing a <u>d</u>izzy <u>d</u>ance.
 An <u>e</u>lephant <u>e</u>ating...

Do you remember all the capital and small letters of the alphabet?
▶ Fill in the missing letters of the alphabet.

A			D	E			H	I		K			N		P	Q				U		W		Y	
	b	c			f	g			j		l	m		o			r	s	t		v		x		z

▶ Write these sets of words in the order of the alphabet.
The first one is done for you.

<u>c</u>amel	<i>ape</i>
<u>a</u>pe	<i>bear</i>
<u>d</u>og	<i>camel</i>
<u>b</u>ear	<i>dog</i>

<u>f</u>ox	
<u>h</u>orse	
<u>g</u>orilla	
<u>e</u>lephant	

<u>m</u>ouse	
<u>r</u>at	
<u>t</u>iger	
<u>p</u>anda	

Alphabetical order

What's next?

▶ Write the next letter.

1 a b c d _e_____	3 i j k l _____	5 q r s t _____
2 e f g h _____	4 m n o p _____	6 u v w x _____

Which letter comes **first** in the alphabet?

▶ Write the letters in the beads in alphabetical order.

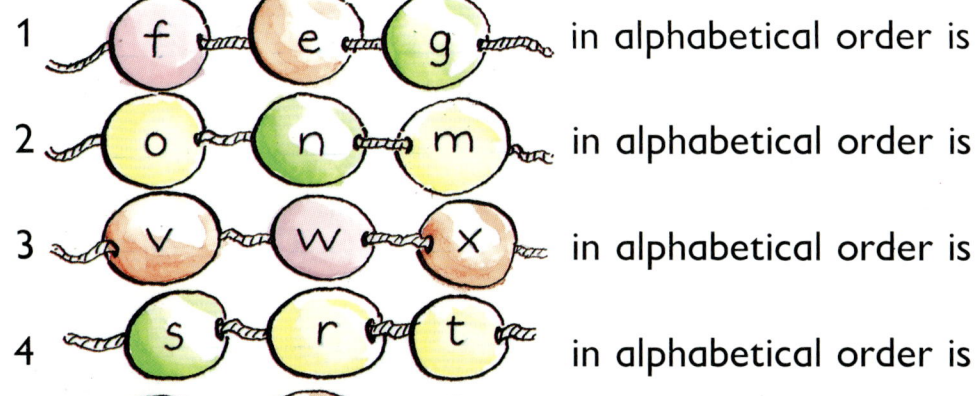

1 f e g   in alphabetical order is   e f g

2 o n m   in alphabetical order is

3 v w x   in alphabetical order is

4 s r t   in alphabetical order is

5 p q r   in alphabetical order is

Have you read: **The Just So Stories?**
Write **yes** or **no** in here. ☐

Write the title of the book you are reading this week.

The alphabet

Look around inside your home for names of things. Look out of the window for more words.

▶ Make your own **Alphabet Zig-Zag**.

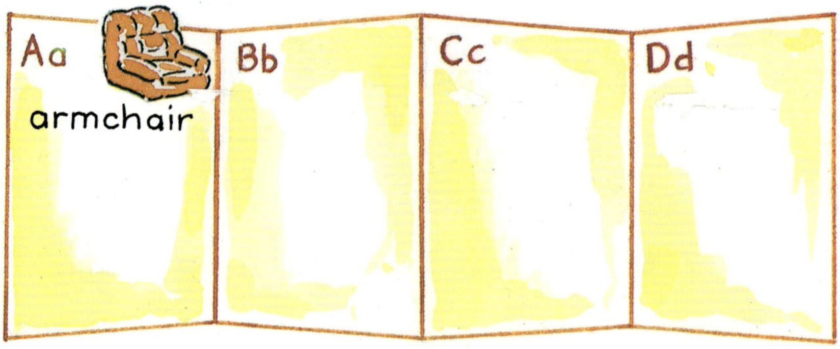

Aa armchair Bb Cc Dd

Ee Ff Gg Hh horse Ii Jj

Kk Ll Mm milkbottle Nn Oo Pp

Qq Rr robin Ss Tt Uu Vv umbrella

Ww worm Xx Yy Zz